DEDICATION

Dedicated to everything I hate or hated.

I love you!

And if I don't, may this story help.

What if hate could be a word,
more pretty like a hummingbird?

That did not hurt or divide.
Or make me want to run and hide.

He, she, they, boy or girl,
it's hard to hate while you whirl!

A feeling that I'm not proud of,
that is the opposite of love.

Before I use that sad word 'hate',
I've been told, that it's best to wait.

And try to use another word,
like dislike or bother, to be heard.

One thing I've noticed about hate,
Hate doesn't like to roller skate!

But sometimes I still feel angry.
Which is normal my friends tell me.

Hate's an emotion that we feel,
and when we do, it feels so real.

But there is something you should know.
Our feelings like to come and go.

Some see different and just hate.
Some see different as just great!

People often say "Don't hate!"
but there are things that don't feel great.

I used to hate both eggs and cheese.
Now when they're served, I say "Yes please!"

Another thing I used to hate,
is when I had to wait...wait...wait.

To some, mornings can be the worst.
They want to wake up and just curse!

And when a bully picked on me,
I'd feel both hate and hurt you see.

Hate can make me feel so mad!
But in some time mad turns to sad.

Now, when I hear or feel hate,
I see if I can make it great.

Like a frown turned
upside down,

I try and turn
anger around.

Now, I'm not just saying that hate,
will go away and you'll feel great.

But hate is something we can choose.
Politely tell hate, "sorry you lose"!

I read and learned when I was 8,
that only LOVE can conquer HATE.

Now, when hate gets thought or said,
I try to understand instead.

How would you like to pledge with me,
to see hate, as well... just silly?

So "goodbye hate" because in the end,
I choose love to be my friend.

Author Books

Be sure to check out other fun and spirited children's books
by author Eric DeSio available at www.BeYouBooks.com

Made in the USA
Middletown, DE
20 October 2022

13070870R00015

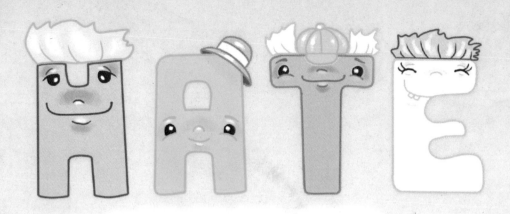

A children's book about 'hate'?

Let's take the power away from the word hate!

What if hate could be a word more pretty like a hummingbird?
That did not hurt or divide or make me want to run and hide.
He, she, they, boy or girl, it's hard to hate while you whirl!
But sometimes I still feel angry. Which is normal, my friends tell me.
Now when I hear or feel hate, I see if I can make it great.

How would you like to pledge with me
to see hate, as well... just silly?

Written by Eric DeSio
Illustrated by Jessica Gamboa
www.BeYouBooks.com

ISBN 9781952637438
90000
9 781952 637438